STARLINGS

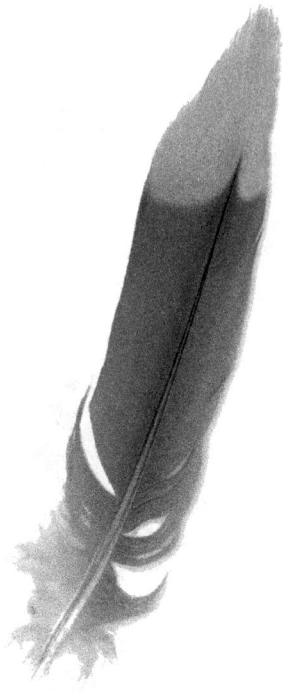

STARLINGS

Black-headed Starling
India

Rose-colored Starling
Europe and Asia

Golden-crowned Starling
India

Pied Starling or Pied Myna
India

Oxpecker or Tick Bird
Africa

Common Starling ~ Citizen of the World ~ Native of Europe and Asia and North Africa ~ Naturalized in South Africa, Australia, and America ~~~

Cockscomb or Masked Starling
Africa

*Written and Illustrated
by WILFRID S. BRONSON*

SUNSTONE PRESS

SANTA FE

Sunstone books may be purchased for educational, business, or sales promotional use. For information please write: Special Markets Department, Sunstone Press, P.O. Box 2321, Santa Fe, New Mexico 87504-2321.

Library of Congress Cataloging-in-Publication Data

Bronson, Wilfrid S. (Wilfrid Swancourt), 1894-
  Starlings / written & illustrated by Wilfrid Swancourt Bronson.
    p. cm.
  Originally published: New York : Harcourt Brace, 1948.
  ISBN 978-0-86534-649-9 (softcover : alk. paper)
  1. Starlings--Juvenile literature. 2. Birds--Juvenile literature. I. Title.

QL696.P278B76 2008
598.8'63--dc22

                          2008000129

Published in

WWW.SUNSTONEPRESS.COM
SUNSTONE PRESS / POST OFFICE BOX 2321 / SANTA FE, NM 87504-2321 /USA
(505) 988-4418 / ORDERS ONLY (800) 243-5644 / FAX (505) 988-1025

STARLINGS

When the singing time of other birds has ended, when
many have flown away, starlings stay with us and still sing.
All through the year, in good weather and bad, in town or
country, a starling will sing. He sings for many minutes at
a time, and many times a day. With a steady stream of soft
gurgling sounds he mixes every now and then a single

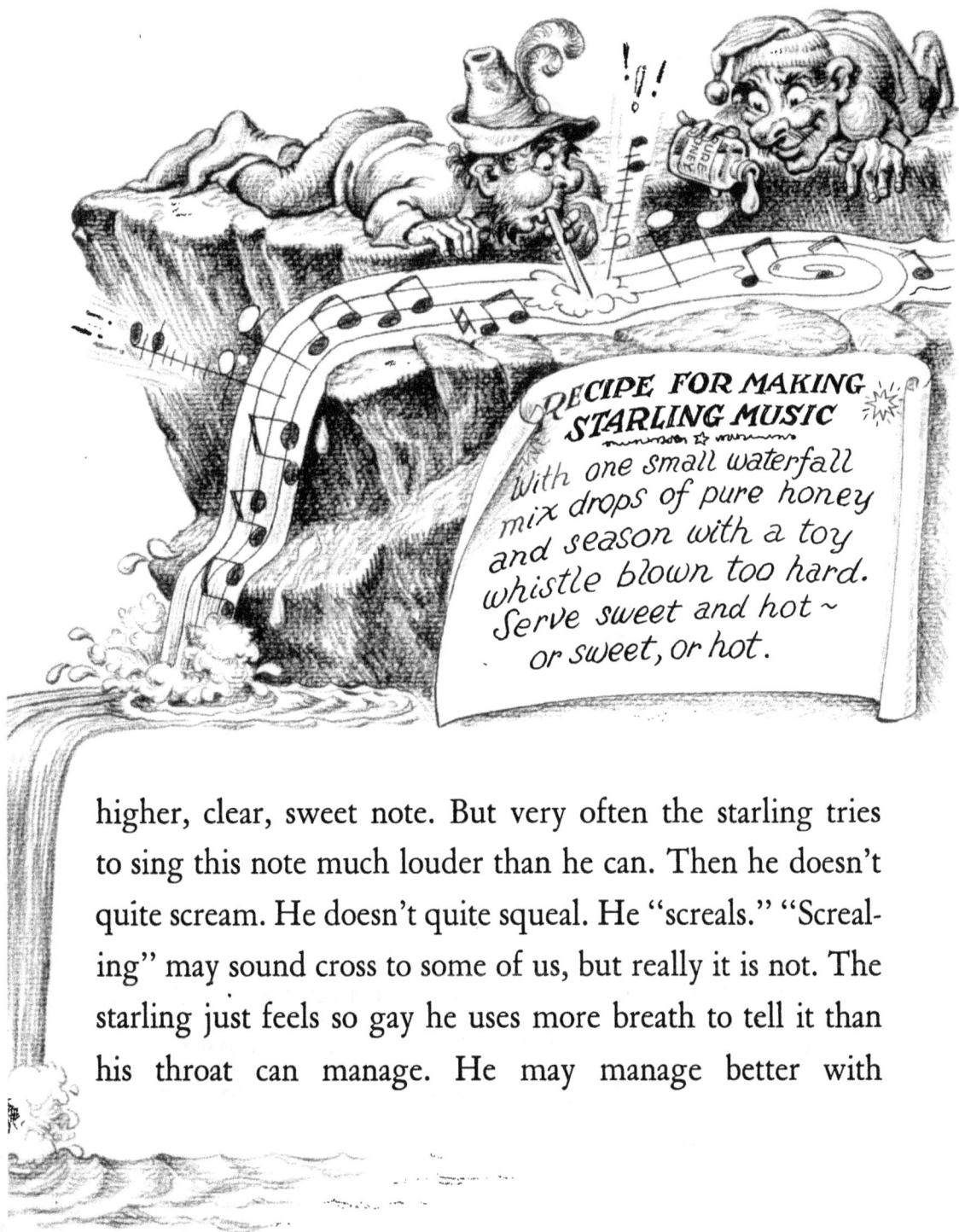

RECIPE FOR MAKING
STARLING MUSIC

With one small waterfall
mix drops of pure honey
and season with a toy
whistle blown too hard.
Serve sweet and hot ~
or sweet, or hot.

higher, clear, sweet note. But very often the starling tries to sing this note much louder than he can. Then he doesn't quite scream. He doesn't quite squeal. He "screals." "Screaling" may sound cross to some of us, but really it is not. The starling just feels so gay he uses more breath to tell it than his throat can manage. He may manage better with

BOB WHITE!
CHICKADEE-DEE-DEE
CLUCK-CLUCK
CA-DA-CUT!

MORTIMER!
CAW! CAW!
PEE-WEEEE!
TUT-TUT!
EE-O-LEEEE

The Virtuoso

the songs and calls of other birds. For many starlings are good mimics. Pet starlings sometimes learn to whistle easy tunes and even to talk a little. Some sing ever so sweetly when they are only one month old.

AS A FLOCK SETTLES DOWN TO SLEEP, ALL TALKING AT ONCE, THE SOUND FROM THEIR MANY STRAIGHT SHARP BILLS IS LIKE 10,000 SWISHING SCISSORS

SUNSET CITY SHEARS & CUTLERY CO. Inc.

Mockingbird

STARLING CHILDREN SINGING:

Their voices are still very soft. Tilting their heads, they seem to listen to themselves. The delicate notes are like those of a mockingbird singing far away.

It is fun to watch such active, bustling birds, although they make trouble for us sometimes. But even then they do not mean to be a bother. When starlings eat the farmer's cherries or his strawberries, they don't know the fruit belongs to him. They only know that they could feed themselves and their families much better if the farmer would

leave them alone. If they eat some of the grain the farmer sows, they don't know they are undoing his hard work. They are simply eating seeds.

In the same way they don't know they are *helping* the farmer when they walk about his hay fields eating weed seeds. They only know he lets them do it. To a bird a seed is a seed, a field is a field.

Why the farmer scares them from one field and not from another will always be a mystery to starlings.

WHY DID HE DO IT?
The Great Farmer Mystery

Starlings do help in the hay fields, for they eat there even in winter when other birds have gone. It seems a wonder that a single weed seed is left by spring, or any insects either.

For actually starlings feed far more on insects than they do on fruit or even seeds. And they find many more insects than those that are in sight. They really rummage for them, poking their strong sharp bills between grass roots, into holes and cracks, and under sticks and stones.

In wintertime, in the country, a few starlings sleep in old barns and sheds, but more of them seek shelter from the cold in dense evergreens. Still more fly in large flocks to towns and cities every night, where they have many clever ways of keeping warm. Every morning these birds fly back to the

THEY SLEEP AMONG THE BULBS OF

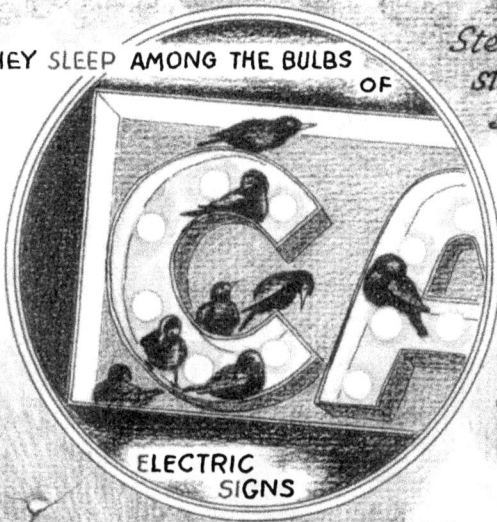

ICE

ELECTRIC SIGNS

Steel chimney stacks are fine stoves, guy-wires good perches. »——→

Atop house chimneys, starlings share the warmth of our fire-places.

OR IN BRANCHES ABOVE STREET LIGHTS.

country, ten, twenty, even thirty miles away, to feed in the fields. When a flock reaches a likely field, some birds sail in for a landing, some fly on a little farther, while others side-

slip to the right and left. Thus when all are down, they are
so spread out that each one can look for seeds and insects
without getting in each other's way.

Just before sunset, with stomachs full, they all flock back to town. Some fly to favorite resting places inside tall church towers. To them the steeple of a rough stone church is just rough stone. But it offers them the refuge of a mighty rock, safety from all enemies of sleeping birds, and from harsh weather. And this is very nice.

If you could open the steeple for a look inside ~

But all the birds don't sleep inside the towers and steeples. And that's where the trouble begins. To birds, trees along city sidewalks are still trees and proper perching places. The sidewalks themselves are just stony ground. But a few thousand starlings, perching all night and every night in city trees, make sidewalks, parked cars, and even people's clothing most untidy.

SHOOSH!

Even though the birds aren't trying to be pests, people have to keep their cities clean. And they have tried in many

On building ledges, people have tried:
living owls
stuffed owls
wire netting
slanting wooden blocks
spikes
noise machines
POW!
BAM!

ways to drive away pigeons and sparrows and starlings when there are too many. But oftentimes it has all been useless or

Foosh!

traps

toy balloons

nearly so. The starlings have left one part of town only to settle in another. Sometimes people have had to shoot them with guns until too few were left to be a nuisance any more. Then very poor folks in the city have dined like that king in Mother Goose, who was served with "four and twenty blackbirds baked in a pie."

shaking trees

BOONG!

fire hoses

cannon crackers

Roman candles

ROBIN
(Likes cherries)

CROW

BOBO~LINK
(Likes rice)

That isn't the end of starling troubles. But let's remember that, like ourselves, starlings are partly good and only partly bad. They aren't the only birds which sometimes bother people and other birds. Robins, bobolinks, and other favorite songbirds worry many a farmer. Crows and grackles, though they eat insects, steal a lot of corn and also eat the eggs of other birds.

RED-WINGED
BLACKBIRD
(*Likes
corn*)

STARLING

GRACKLE

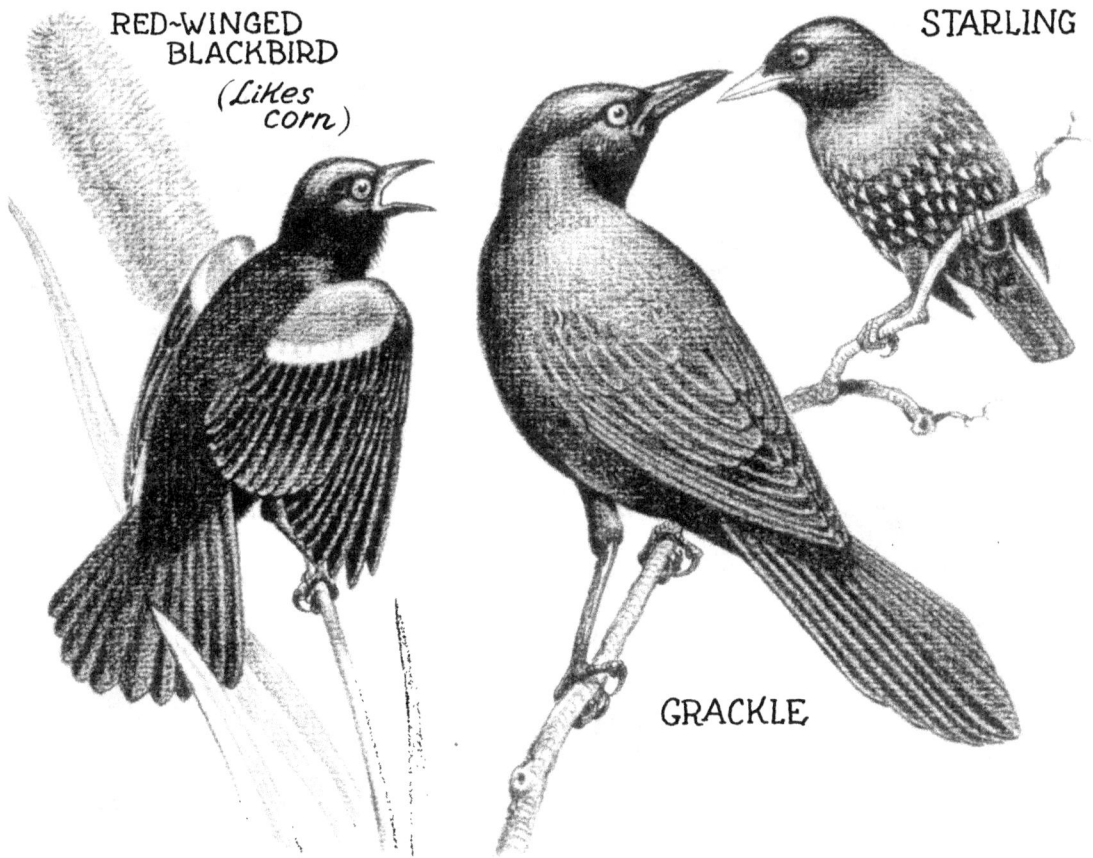

Sometimes starlings are blamed for things the grackles do. So we must be careful not to get the birds confused. Grackles are bigger than starlings, have long tails, and are black all over. Starlings have short tails and yellow bills, and they don't care so much for corn. Often when they flock to the cornfields, it is to eat the Japanese beetles, not the corn.

Though starlings do not rob the nests of other birds, they often make their own nests where other birds would like to build, in holes in old trees, holes in old barns, holes in boxes put up for birds by people. But since starlings can barely get through any hole less than one and three-quarters inches wide, that leaves holes one and one-half inches wide or smaller for swallows, bluebirds, chickadees, nuthatches, wrens, and other hole-nesting birds smaller than the starlings.

Flickers, or High-holes, or
Yellow-hammers,
or Yuckers

LET ME
TAKE A
WHACK
AT IT.

Woodpeckers, especially flickers, probably have the greatest starling trouble. For while a flicker pair is *pecking* out a hole in a tree (with a nice round door over two inches wide), several starling pairs may be *picking* it out for their own. Not a starling tries to move in till the work is all done, but then they all try. The flickers can fight off one pair of starlings easily. But for every pair they chase away, another pair moves in, until the tired flickers give up and start a new hole somewhere else.

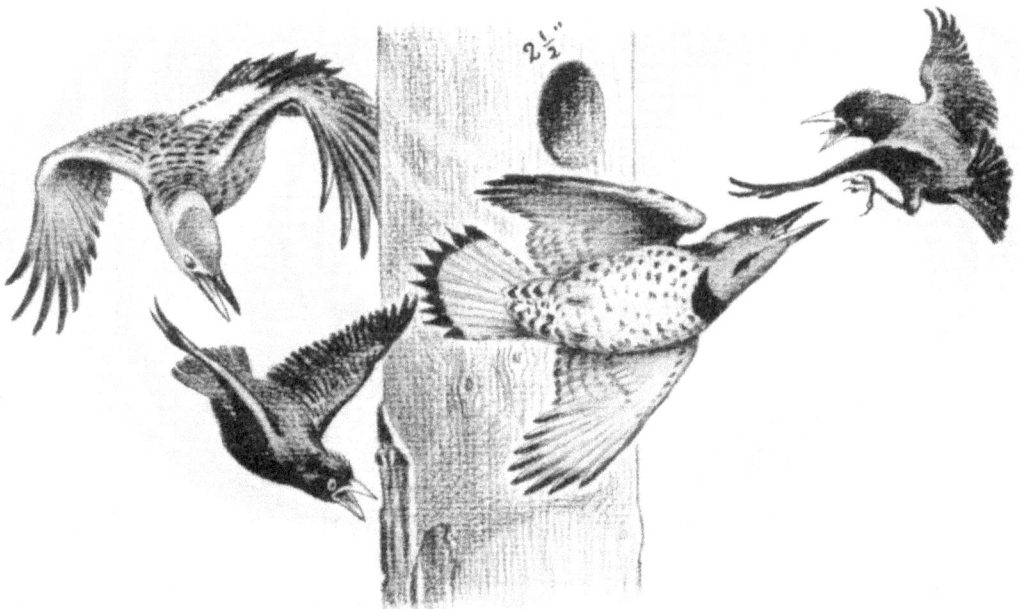

2½"

Sometimes, if the flickers return after starlings move in, they can tackle that pair alone and win back their home.

PEACE AND HARMONY:
Every bird here has the kind
of nesting place it wants.
No bird wants what any of
the others have.

ORIOLE

CATBIRD

SONG SPARROW

However, with the many kinds of birds that don't use holes for nesting-places, starlings get along quite peaceably.

STARLING

ROBIN

Some people think that starlings have no right to food or nesting-places because they are not "American birds." Yet all the starlings you see were born in America. So were their parents and grandparents and great-great-grandparents and all their relatives clear back to 1890. In that year their ancestors were caught in Europe and brought in cages to America. So many American birds had been killed at that time by our own ancestors that our crops were growing wormier and wormier each year, while insect pests grew worse and worse. So starlings were imported to help us fight the insects. They were freed in Central Park in New York City and left to look out for themselves.

A Bird's-eye View

I SAY! IT LOOKS AWFULLY WIDE!

WELL, HERE'S WHERE THEY SET US FREE.
LET'S STAY IN THIS LAND OF LIBERTY.

LONG ISLAND
JAMAICA BAY
BROOKLYN
NEW YORK CITY

Now starlings are just as able to find their way back home as homing pigeons are. But none of them could fly clear back across the ocean. So they had to stay and try to succeed here in America. And, being intelligent birds, they succeeded very well. Every spring new pairs, born in America, moved farther out of the city, seeking places for their own first nests. And every summer, when nesting time was over, starlings young and old gathered in bigger and bigger flocks and flew farther and farther, looking for more feeding grounds and roosting places.

So they spread, until today there are starlings from Canada to Texas, and all across this country from the Atlantic seashore to the Rocky Mountains. Many of those in Canada come back to us each fall. Winters are too cold for them up there, and food is harder to find, especially garbage. There are more towns and cities here, and probably more good food is thrown away in our own United States than anywhere else on earth. People who think that starlings should be starvelings because they are "foreigners" should remember that these American-born birds save much of what they themselves throw away and are still helping us to fight insects as they did in 1890.

TO GET ALONG, YOU MUST BE ABLE TO CHANGE YOUR WAYS AT TIMES.

SO, SINCE INSECTS AND SEEDS ARE SCARCE NOW, WE'LL EAT GARBAGE.

THESE PICTURES SHOW WHY AMERICAN BIRDS BECAME
SO SCARCE. WHILE WASTEFUL PEOPLE WERE KILLING
MILLIONS OF DUCKS, GEESE, AND OTHER GAME-BIRDS
FOR "FUN", OTHERS SHOT NESTING HERONS FOR THEIR

MANY WOMEN THOUGHT THE
PLUMES LOOKED BETTER ON
THEMSELVES THAN ON THE BIRDS.

"very smart"

I ALSO USED
THEM TO DUST
MY FURNITURE
AND TO SHOO
FLIES.

"out of this world"

Knock over
everything big
enough to make
a mouthful!

MEAT MARKET

PLUMES WHILE STILL OTHERS KILLED MILLIONS OF SONG~
BIRDS TO SELL FOR MEAT. AT LAST, WISER PEOPLE MADE
LAWS TO STOP SUCH THINGS AND BROUGHT STARLINGS
TO REPLACE THE INSECT~EATING BIRDS WE HAD LOST.

SO LET'S BE FAIR. IF AMERICAN-BORN STARLINGS ARE FOREIGNERS, THEN SO ARE ALL PEOPLE BORN IN AMERICA EXCEPT THE INDIANS. SO ARE MANY KINDS OF BIRDS, ANIMALS, AND PLANTS. OUR ANCESTORS BROUGHT THEM HERE FROM OTHER COUNTRIES.

peacocks

parrots

pigeons

canaries

guinea fowls

chickens

pheasants

various ducks, geese, and swans

goldfish

carp

brown trout

oranges, apples, cherries, and many other fruits and vegetables

cattle

horses

goats

sheep

donkeys

pigs

dogs

cats

house-rats, mice, & roaches

BUT IF ALL THESE CREATURES, AND OURSELVES, ARE AMERICAN

NOW, THEN SO ARE THE STARLINGS. YES INDEED!

When we try to imagine beings more splendid than ourselves, we think of angels with feathery wings. But birds do not have to imagine such splendor. Their wings are real. And though nowadays, with wonderful inventions, we can zoom across the sky, birds still are freer than we are to go wherever they wish, whenever they wish to go. If a bird

Let's take off! What's the use of waiting?

wants to fly south in the autumn, it springs into the air and flies south.

KEEPEMUP AIR LINES

WAITING ROOM

You need a pilot, co-pilot, stewardess, and crew.

For a bird is its own airplane, passenger, and pilot all in one. Unlike our great flying machines, a bird is alive and doesn't need expensive fuel to keep it going. It gets its flying-power from its food. It naturally enjoys refueling on its journeys, landing almost anywhere whenever it is hungry.

AS FEW MILES OR AS MANY AT A TIME AS THEY PLEASE~

Um! This was worth stopping for!

A plane, on the other hand, must land at an airport. It must be anchored against strong winds or housed in a hangar. Men must repair or replace worn parts and tune up its engines.

All a traveling bird needs to repair its "engines" is a little rest. A bird's engines are, of course, its flying-muscles. Two

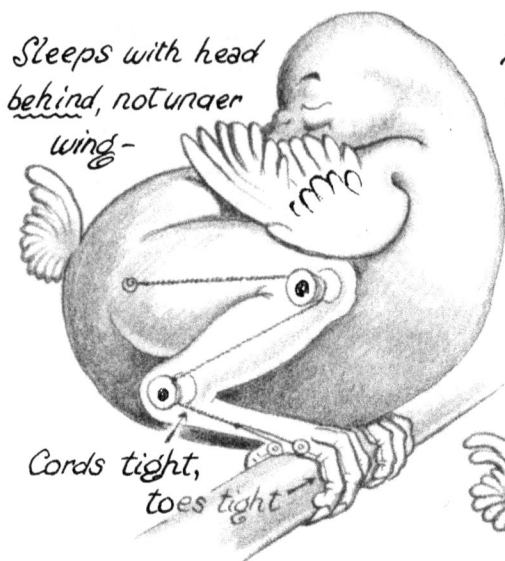

Sleeps with head behind, not under wing -

Cords tight, toes tight

In fact, the bird has to stand up to let go of its perch.

A bird doesn't fall when it sleeps because it has automatic anchors in its legs. When it sits down, cords, pulling over the joints, draw its toes up about the branch.

Cords loose, toes free

sets of breast muscles flap the wings, keeping the bird up and moving along after it springs into the air. The larger

It flies forward under your right thumb, backward under your left.

Up and ready, —

muscles, while reaching forward, press the wings down strongly on the air. The smaller ones, aided by the rush of air as the bird speeds on, move the wings upward and backward, ready for the next flap forward and down by the bigger muscles. A flap is like a leap, with only air to tread on. Look at the little corner pictures one by one; then run the pages under your thumb and you will see a movie of how birds fly by flapping.

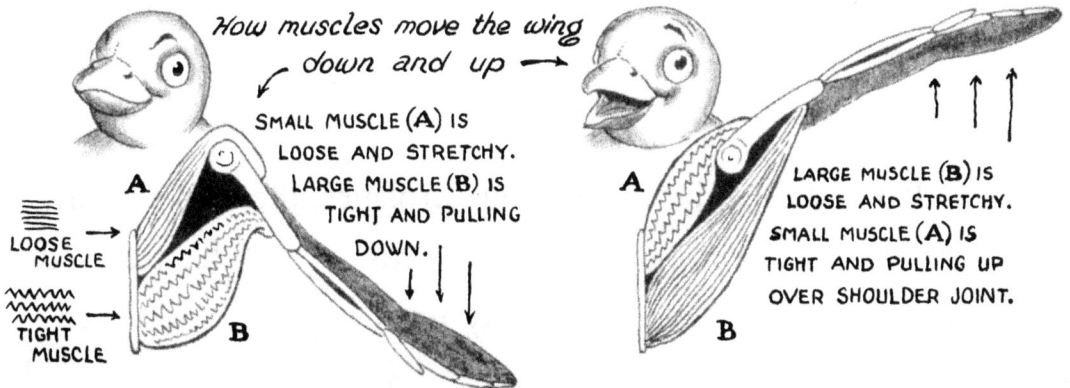

How muscles move the wing down and up →

SMALL MUSCLE (A) IS LOOSE AND STRETCHY. LARGE MUSCLE (B) IS TIGHT AND PULLING DOWN.

A

LOOSE MUSCLE →

TIGHT MUSCLE →

B

LARGE MUSCLE (B) IS LOOSE AND STRETCHY. SMALL MUSCLE (A) IS TIGHT AND PULLING UP OVER SHOULDER JOINT.

A

B

CRUISERS ARE LIKE

EAGLES

AND

ALBATROSSES.

SPEED PLANES ARE LIKE

fast turning

SWALLOWS AND STARLINGS.

HELICOPTERS ARE LIKE

HUMMINGBIRDS

flying in one place, or forward, or backward.

If we say that birds are living airplanes, then just as truly we can call planes big mechanical birds. For we have copied birds in building planes. To fly well, both bird and plane must be streamlined. They must be rounded in front and taper to feather thinness behind, so that they part the air and slip through it with the least disturbance. Each must be strongly made, but light as possible for its size. So a plane's

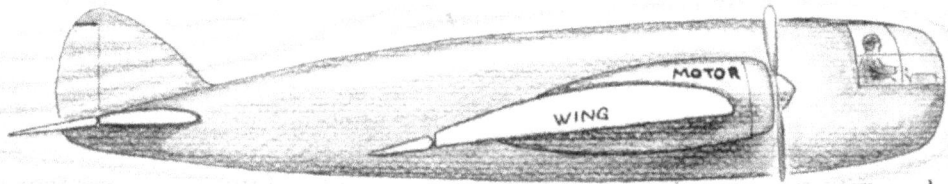

forward and —

Like the plane's body, its wings and motors are streamlined. So are the bird's.

MOTOR

WING

The plane's "flying-muscles" are the motors in its wings.

The pilot is the plane's brain — in its head.

AIR CLOSING

AIR PARTING

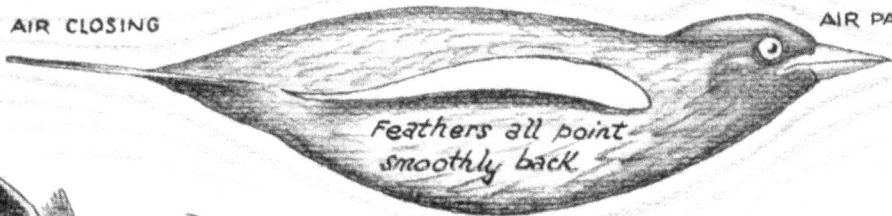

Feathers all point smoothly back

"Landing gear" of birds is retracted among the breast feathers.

Planes also draw their "legs" up out of the way.

wings are hollow except for the braces in them. A bird's wings are hollow too, though in a different way. The stems or shafts of all the feathers are hollow, flexible as fishing rods, and very strong for anything so light.

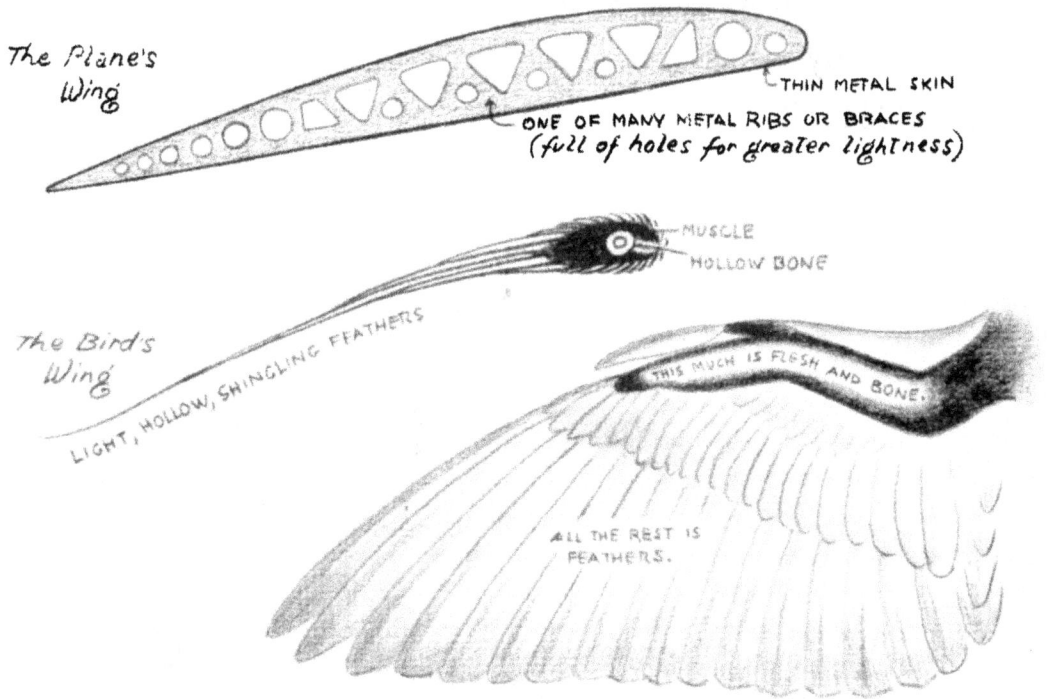

The Plane's Wing

THIN METAL SKIN

ONE OF MANY METAL RIBS OR BRACES
(full of holes for greater lightness)

MUSCLE

HOLLOW BONE

The Bird's Wing

LIGHT, HOLLOW, SHINGLING FEATHERS

THIS MUCH IS FLESH AND BONE.

ALL THE REST IS FEATHERS.

Instead of arms or front legs, the bird has wings. But the form and size of a wing is made up mostly of the light, hollow feathers. And more than that, in the wings of many kinds of birds, some of the bones are hollow. There is air

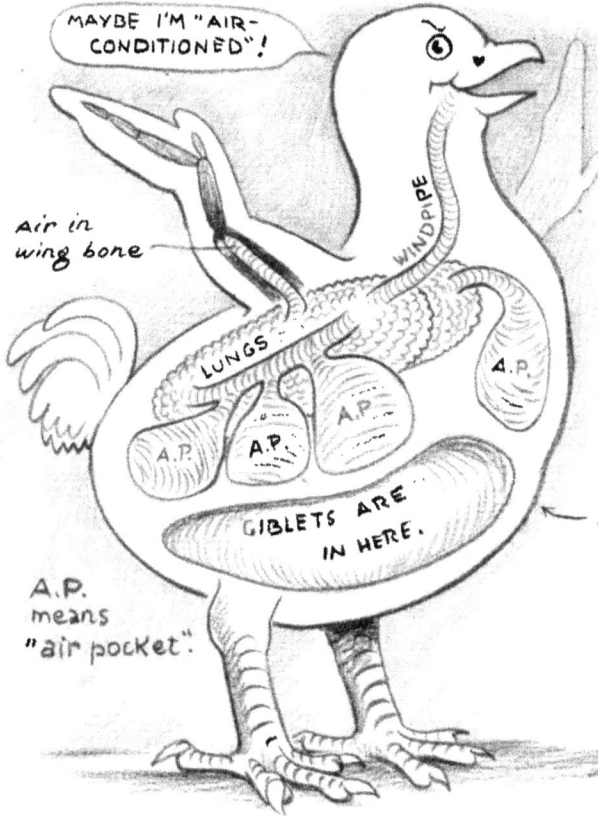

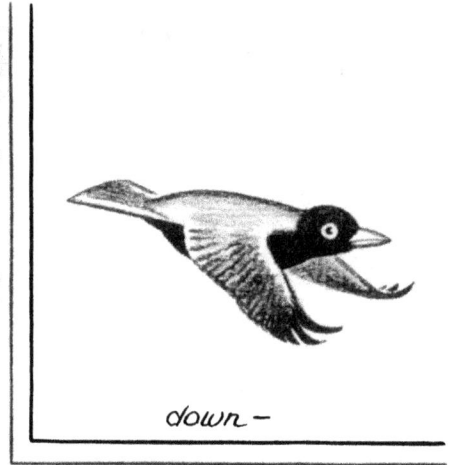

This picture is only meant to show how pockets, lungs, and hollow bones are connected and filled with air through the windpipe of a bird.

in these bones, and there are pockets of air in a bird's body, connected with the air in the bones and in the lungs.

The bird is lighter than it would be if these spaces were filled up with fat and marrow, and this must help it in flying. Perhaps having air all through its body keeps it from getting overheated with the exercise of flying. For birds cannot perspire to keep cool. They aren't water-cooled like people, but air-cooled like many airplane engines.

HOW EGGS ARE MADE IN THE GREAT FLYING BIRD FACTORY:

(Just about the same thing happens in real birds.)

A yolk starts along the egg passage. It stops and is wound in layers of "white". It moves on and →

MATERIALS

Engine Room

MATERIAL CONVERTING CHAMBER

(Fuel and Egg Ingredients)

YOLK STORAGE ROOM

PATENTS APPLIED FOR: W.S.B

The great mechanical birds, our planes produced in factories, can't reproduce themselves. But birds are their own plane factories.

stops for a layer of lime. This hardens
and becomes the shell. The egg
goes on and gets a coat of color
(unless the bird lays white eggs). Then
it moves once more, out of the bird, into
the nest.

- ward - -

EGG WHITE

SHELL DEPARTMENT

Coating

Drying

WINDING
DEPARTMENT

LIQUID
LIME

PAINTING
ROOM

BLUE

PALE
GREEN

BROWN

BLACK

TO HEAT-TREATING PLA

In the nest it is heat-treated,
kept very warm, until it hatches.
One more bird!

Every egg a bird lays is a wondrous package holding all
things needed to produce another bird, another living airplane.

Before any eggs are laid, birds must prepare their nests. When we see some of the beautiful nests they make we wonder how such work could possibly be done without a pair of skillful hands. But there is plenty of skill in a bird's bill, though of course some birds are more talented than others. Starlings are only middling good nest builders. Since they always build in some cozy hole, they need not be as skillful as a bird that builds out in the branches of a tree.

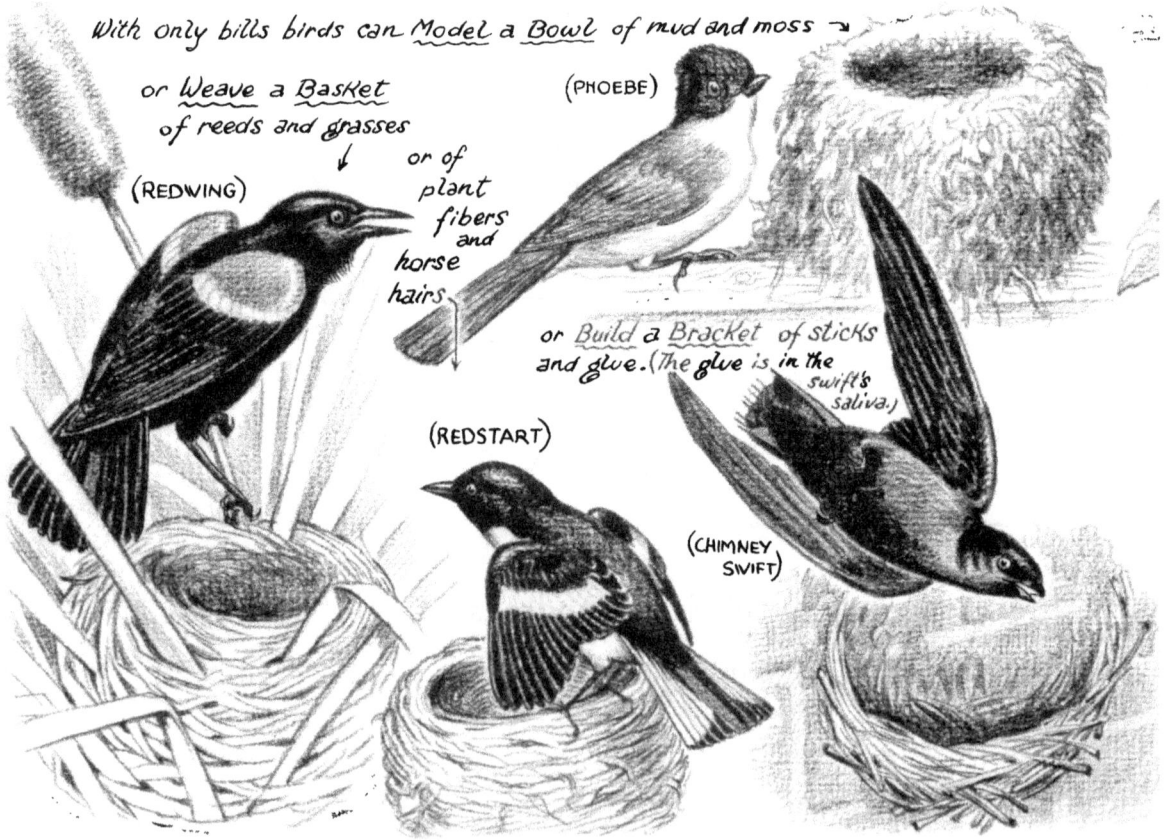

With only bills birds can _Model_ a _Bowl_ of mud and moss

or _Weave_ a _Basket_ of reeds and grasses

(PHOEBE)

(REDWING)

or of plant fibers and horse hairs

or _Build_ a _Bracket_ of sticks and glue. (The glue is in the swift's saliva.)

(REDSTART)

(CHIMNEY SWIFT)

They can *Carve a Vase in wood* or

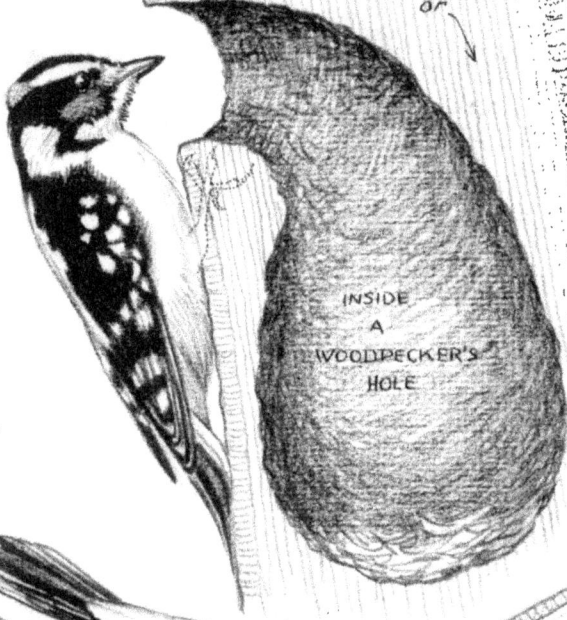

INSIDE
A
WOODPECKER'S
HOLE

upward

Model a Vase of clay.

(CLIFF or EAVES SWALLOW)

(ORIOLE)

They can *Knit a Bag* of string, horse-hair grasses etc., or *Form a Cup* of thistledown, mosses, and spider's silk.

(HUMMINGBIRD)

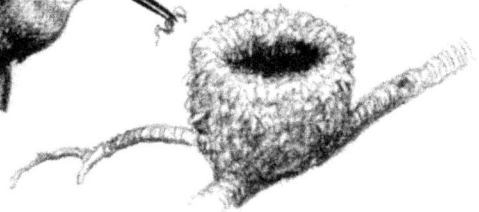

7 POSES OF
1 STARLING
SINGING IN
THE SPRING

and backward

First of all, any male starling that wants to be married has to find a good nest-hole. He may have kept an eye on one and sung close by it all winter long. But in the early spring he begins to sing beside it for hours every day, as loudly as he can. He twitches his wings and bulges his throat till the feathers there stand out like a bristly beard. He swings his body from side to side, as though he had a mighty audience before him. Then he flips about and faces the other way as though there were an audience behind him too.

Though most of his audience may be out of sight, he doesn't mind as long as other birds, especially other starlings, listen. Not even all other starlings are required to lend an ear. Any starlings which already have their mates and nests may go about their business. But to other bachelors like himself, or to any starling pairs which have no nesting places, his song keeps saying,

"Stay away from this nest-hole and the grounds around it! They're my private property!"

The same notes carry a very different message to unmated females. They say,

"Come, one of you, and be my wife! Come here and see what a splendid nest-hole I am saving for you!"

OH BLISS !
A WIFE
AT LAST !

Once in a while he stops singing to look for food. And he may carry into the hole a few sticks, straws, chicken feathers, or anything else that's handy. But he won't go far in his search for food or nest materials, lest other starlings occupy the hole. And he does not want to be far away if a lady starling comes in answer to his invitation.

Sooner or later a female comes along, and if she likes the nest-hole she is almost sure to be his bride. The kind of place he offers seems more important to her than how grand he looks or how well he sings. The first thing she does, if she decides to stay—and she usually does—is to pitch out everything he has collected in the hole.

Perhaps she feels that housekeeping is her own affair and that her husband has only muddled things up in spite of his good intentions. This doesn't discourage him at all. Bit by bit he will pick up the pieces and carry them into the hole again. But now she is in charge and can arrange the stuff to

Stripping a cedar post-

suit herself. They both get more materials, working off and on for about a week, mostly in the mornings and late afternoons. Besides long straws, thin twigs, and chicken feathers, they pull thin strips of bark from cedar trees or fence posts. Perhaps the smell of cedar keeps bird lice away. If so, this bark is doubly useful in the nest.

If you're through for the day —
Let's go! What say?

O.K! Why stay?
Let's both get away!

ONE FOR THE MONEY —
TWO FOR THE SHOW —
THREE! AND AWAY
TO THE FIELDS THEY GO.

When the nest is ready, the first egg is laid, the same turquoise blue-green as a robin's egg, though slightly paler. But neither the mother nor the father bird sits on it. Each morning another egg is added, but the sitting doesn't begin till all the eggs (from four to seven) have been laid. Other-

wise they would not hatch together, since the first egg is laid a week ahead of the last one. And the babies would all be different sizes, each ready to fly on a different day. Such a family would be too hard to feed and care for, so the sitting starts only after every egg is in the nest.

Before settling down, she turns each egg with her bill so that both sides are warmed and aired alike.

Both starling parents take turns sitting on the eggs, but the mother always takes the night shift. The father may sleep in some favorite cranny near by or he may fly back to the old church steeple where the big flock sleeps in winter. There he has the company of other husbands like himself and very probably of bachelors too.

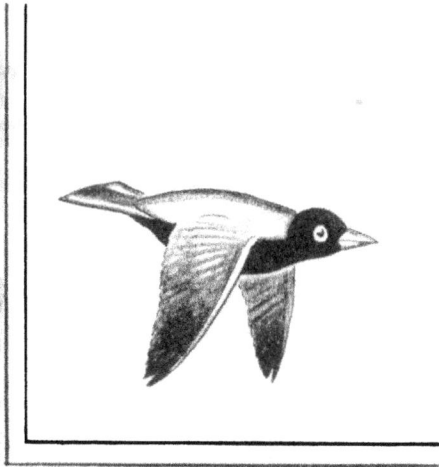

He would have company
in the steeple, but the
old shed is handier.

At the first sign of sunrise he hurries home and sings a gay
good morning to his wife. When she comes out of the hole
he may go right in to take a turn on the eggs. But sometimes
on warm mornings, they fly off together for their breakfast
and a little exercise before he begins his share of work.

By keeping the eggs warm for from twelve to fourteen days, the starling pair brings something very wonderful to pass. For now, instead of yolks and whites, each egg contains a baby bird.

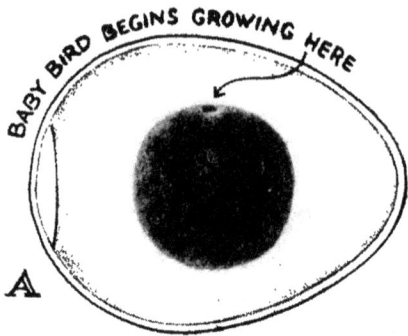

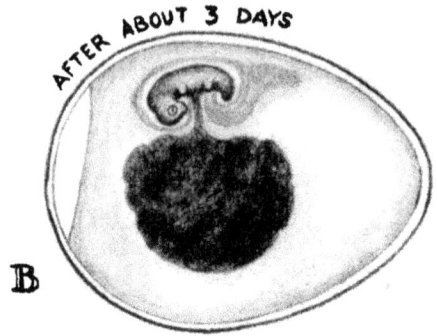

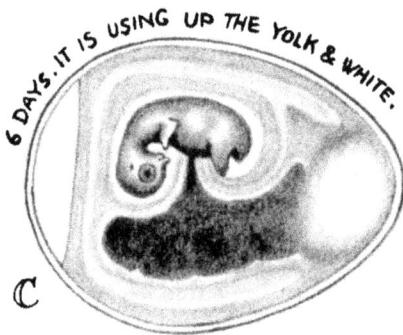

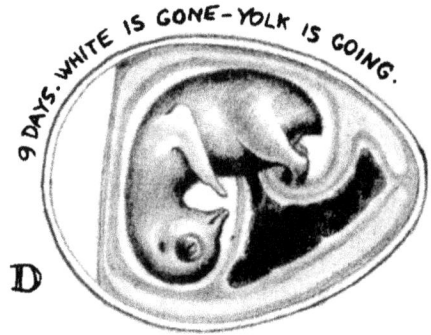

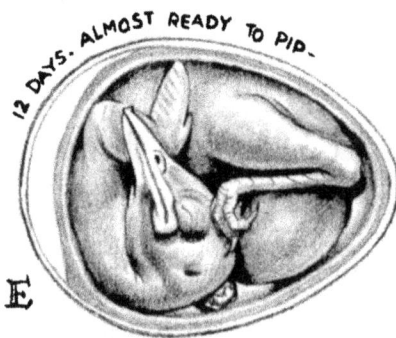

BABY BIRD BEGINS GROWING HERE

A

AFTER ABOUT 3 DAYS

B

6 DAYS. IT IS USING UP THE YOLK & WHITE.

C

9 DAYS. WHITE IS GONE - YOLK IS GOING.

D

12 DAYS. ALMOST READY TO PIP -

E

PIPPING BEGINS

F

The hard, sharp pipping tooth →

A baby songbird hatches sooner than a baby chicken. But it isn't cute and downy nor ready to run about and feed itself. It cannot open its eyes. It is too weak to do anything but open its mouth for food.

Every baby bird in its egg has one tooth with which to begin its life. It is right on the end of the bill. The bill itself is much too soft for pecking through the shell at hatching time. But the baby needs air and food and room if it is to live and grow. So, with its one tooth, it pecks and pecks till the shell cracks open a little way, letting in the air. Soon it tries to stretch its folded wings and legs, and this breaks the shell wide open. And, having done its work, the pipping tooth drops from the bill.

The old birds carry out the empty eggshells and drop them after flying well away. They hunt for insects, especially

juicy caterpillars, to feed the family. All day long, every few minutes, one or the other comes back with a beakful of food for the children. It isn't hard for them to tell whose turn is next. For when a baby's stomach is full, more food just won't go down its throat. So mamma takes the caterpillar from the mouth (still open like the rest) and pops it into a hungrier one.

Though a nest-hole often is an extremely hot and thirsty place, the babies never get a drink. All the water they need

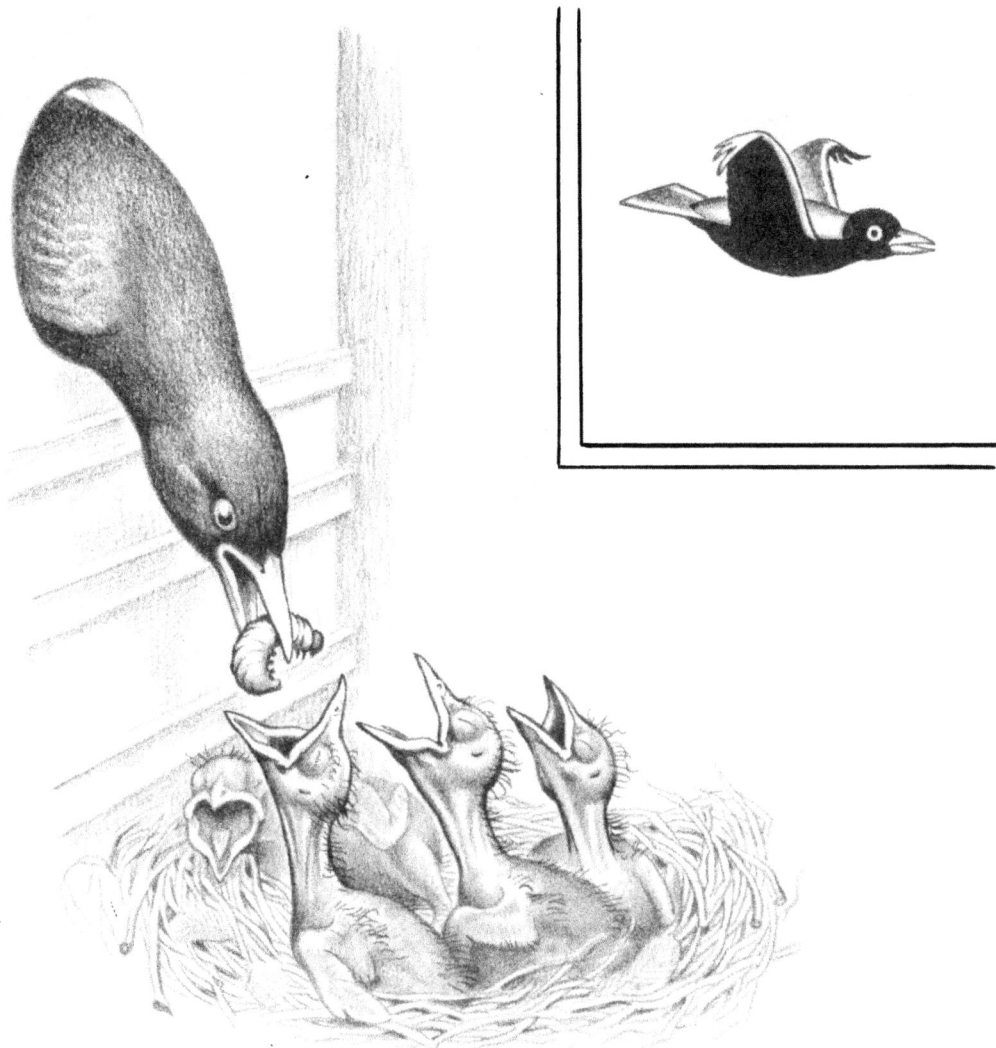

is in their food, in fruit, and caterpillars. This wouldn't be enough if baby birds lost any precious water by perspiring or by making puddles, but they don't. They only make little white bundles which the parents carry away and drop, as they did the eggshells.

For the first few nights the mother starling sleeps with her children. But soon they are big enough to keep each other warm, and she rests better roosting somewhere else.

PERHAPS SHE JOINS HER HUSBAND IN THE BROKEN-DOWN OLD SHED.

These are very hard-working days for her and her husband. They must catch thousands of insects every day to keep up with their babies' appetites and their own. Only now and then can the father starling find a moment for a song.

Starlings eat many insects that are bad for our gardens, orchards, grain-fields, lawns, parks, etc. Baby starlings are fed baby insects (mostly soft, smooth caterpillars) such as:

GRUB-WORMS, CUT-WORMS, INCH-WORMS, TOMATO, AND WIRE WORMS.

Grown-up starlings eat grown-up insects (many with hard shells) such as:

CLICK, MAY, POTATO, BEAN, & JAPANESE BEETLES;

also

WEEVILS, ANTS, GRASS-HOPPERS, & CRICKETS;

and

HUNDRED-LEGS, THOUSAND-LEGS, & SPIDERS,

as well as

SLUGS & BUFFALO BUGS

AND MANY, MANY OTHERS.

The babies grow rapidly. Their eyes are open now. Their beaks are hardening except at the corners where the lips stay soft and stretchy, allowing their mouths to open very wide. They all whisper, "Swizzleswizzleswiss!" whenever a parent bird comes near.

About one week old.
Plenty of pin-feathers
on the babies now.

A PIN-FEATHER IS REALLY ONLY A FEATHER CASE. THE REAL FEATHER GROWS INSIDE IT. AT FIRST IT IS POINTED, — LIKE A PIN.

BUT SOON THE END OPENS AND OUT COMES THE REAL FEATHER TIP, — LIKE A PAINT-BRUSH.

WHEN THE FEATHER IS NEARLY GROWN, THE PIN-FEATHER CASE CRACKS AND FALLS OFF.

$\frac{1}{2}$ GROWN.

About two weeks old.

They are restless in the nest and take turns climbing up to peer out of the door. The one at the door shuts off the light and air from his brothers and sisters, and, if he stays there too long, they may jostle him till he drops back into the nest. Thus all get a little exercise and learn a bit about the world outside.

NOW, WHICHEVER YOUNGSTER IS IN THE DOORWAY, GETS THE FOOD.

Soon there is rarely a moment when the baby starlings are not staring out of the door. Watching their parents and other birds fly seems to make them ever more eager to try it themselves. They stand up in the nest, stretch their legs, and fan their short-feathered wings. But starlings are successful birds partly because they keep their children in the nest until they are really ready to fly. Very seldom will you find a baby starling fluttering weakly along the ground with half-grown feathers, a ready meal for cat or dog.

About _three_ weeks old.

STRETCHING

Young starlings, ready to fly but still in the nest.

Young robin, out of the nest a little too soon.

Once out of the nest, babies never go back, but perch in the trees calling, "I'm here!" every now and then, lest they get lost and hungry. For they must be fed another ten days or so before they learn to feed themselves. Other things come more quickly, for birds are born almost knowing how to fly, to drink, to bathe, to preen their feathers, and so on.

To light gently at 50 miles an hour: coast and →

How to wipe the bill

after learning to drink —

How to bathe and shake to dry —

How to use one wing as a prop, put a leg over it, and

scratch the head,

and to roll the head the while.

Fencing: Fun crossing bills –

roll back shoulders, lower tail, and coast uphill to branch. Or, to light easily on the ground, lower tail and back-flap rapidly.

To squeeze "the last thing over the fence" to get oil to put on the feathers, to comb them with the bill, and to manicure the legs.

There isn't room in a nest for a frolic. But now the young birds have the whole sky for their fun, chasing and learning to dodge each other, cutting fancy capers, coasting down an invisible hill of wind, turning to face it and climb again, and flying as a flock with their parents.

PERHAPS THE PARENT BIRDS ARE PROUD OF THEIR NEW FAMILY. CERTAINLY THEY ARE HAPPY TO BE FLYING WITH THEM. FOR NOW THE HARD NESTING CHORES ARE OVER. AND STARLINGS ARE VERY SOCIABLE. THEY LIKE TO BE WITH OTHERS.

LONG AGO, WHEN EVERYTHING WAS WILD, INCLUDING PEOPLE,
PIGEONS AND STARLINGS NESTED IN THE SAME CRAGS AND
CLIFFS IN EUROPE. TODAY WILD STARLINGS STILL LIKE TO
JOIN PIGEONS, (OUR TAME ONES), WHEN THEY EXCERCISE. THE
PIGEONS DO NOT SEEM TO MIND AT ALL. THEY TOO ARE
SOCIABLE, AND STARLINGS ARE OLD-TIME COMPANY. THEY
ALL FLY VERY WELL TOGETHER .

By the middle of June, the little family joins other starling families, forming a flock perhaps of fifty or a hundred birds. Flock joins flock until five hundred or a thousand birds may

Young bills are dark; and old bills are duller in →

be together. It is easy to pick out the young birds. They are entirely brownish-gray except for a dull white throat-piece, very different from the black and glossy adults.

winter than they are in spring and summer.

They drop their feathers
in pairs.

Both
number
one feathers
go first.
When the new
number ones
are about ½
grown, both
number twos
drop out, and
so on.

etc.
5
4
3
2

1

Thus the bird
remains balanced
and able to fly —

2
3
4
5 etc.

1

even while changing its feathers.

But in August, though the young starlings have worn their gray suits for only two months, they get a whole new set of feathers. All starlings, young and old, change costumes at this time each year. They lose just a few feathers at a time, and as fast as they fall out new ones grow.

THE OLD MALE BIRDS ARE SPANGLED, THE OLD FEMALES MORE SO, BUT THE NEW BIRDS MOST OF ALL.

In winter a starling looks like a patch of midnight sky sparkling with little stars.

So perhaps "Starling" is as proper a name for him as "Duckling" is for a little duck, or "Gosling" for a little goose.

When the molt, or feather changing, is complete, the brand-new clothes are truly beautiful. Now every starling, young and old, is wearing glossy black full of purple, green, and blue reflections and spangled with little sparks of white and orange.

OUR STARLINGS HAVE MANY
HANDSOME AND HELPFUL
RELATIVES IN THE
OLD WORLD.

THE BEAUTIFUL ROSE-COLORED STARLINGS, (ROSE WITH BLACK
CRESTED HEAD, BLACK WINGS AND TAIL), COME TO EUROPE
FROM INDIA IN THE SUMMERTIME. THEY EAT MILLIONS OF
LOCUSTS AND FEED THEM ALSO TO THEIR YOUNG ONES. THIS
HELPS TO SAVE THE GROWING CROPS OF THE FARMERS.~

THE OX-PECKERS OR TICK-BIRDS ARE AFRICAN STARLINGS. THEY HELP THE CATTLE, (WILD OR TAME), AS WELL AS ELEPHANTS, RHINOCEROSES, GIRAFFES, AND ANTELOPES BY EATING THE TICKS THAT BOTHER THESE ANIMALS. OUR OWN STARLINGS LIKE TO FEED IN THE FIELDS AMONG THE COWS. ~ ~ ~

In the early autumn the big starling flocks grow even bigger as others join them from Canada. In some places you may see ten thousand birds or more together. Some flocks stay in the country, sleeping among the reeds of marshes till colder weather forces them to seek deep evergreens or to travel south.

MANY STARLINGS LEARNED TO GO SOUTH
FOR THE WINTER BY TRAVELING WITH GRACKLES,
REDWINGS, AND OTHER AMERICAN BLACK-
BIRDS WHICH ALREADY KNEW THE WAY.

Others fly each night to roost among the buildings of our cities. But wherever they spend the winter, starlings sing—under clear skies or gray, when clean white snow is everywhere or dirty slush, in warm spells or in freezing rain.

And when spring comes again at last, there the starlings are, still singing. And there perhaps we had better leave them, singing, singing, singing.

www.ingramcontent.com/pod-product-compliance
Lightning Source LLC
Chambersburg PA
CBHW062032090426
42733CB00034B/2600